MY WARRIOR SON

Battle Letters For Life

My Warrior Son,

_____

_____

_____

_____

_____

_____

_____

_____

"For the LORD your God is the One who goes with you
to fight for you against your enemies
to give you victory."
(Deuteronomy 20:4)

Table of Contents

1. The Frontline
2. Prepare for Battle
3. The Power Prayer
4. Fueled By Faith
5. Run to Win
6. When Life Hits
7. Battlefield of the Mind
8. Truth is Your Armor
9. No Weapon Will Prosper
10. Become Fearless
11. Courage to Change
12. Get Up
13. The Bait of Bitterness
14. Sovereign Suffering
15. A Way of Escape
16. Pick Up Your Cross
17. Identity Crisis
18. Hopelessness Illusion
19. Stand
20. Relational Wars
21. In the Dark
22. Tender Warrior
23. Break Through
24. Not of This World
25. Rebuild
26. Rest for the Warrior
27. Conquer Evil
28. The Power of Purity
29. Amazing Grace
30. Women
31. Praise Through the Pain
32. Born to Lead
33. The Trust Factor
34. The Work Force
35. Breakthrough
36. Driven by Eternity
37. Conquer Compromise
38. Capture This Day
39. The Invisible War
40. Powerless Apart from Me
41. Blessed
42. Release Your Prisoner
43. Count the Cost
44. Don't Underestimate
45. Your Appointed Position
46. Life Without Limits
47. Warrior Wisdom
48. Speak Life!
49. The Legacy
50. It is Finished!

The Frontline

My Warrior Son,

More than ever, I need you to willingly walk to the frontline and fight! You were born to become a hero whether you believe it or not. There is a deep desire inside your soul to conquer something great. I know this because I am the one who placed it there. The only thing that is holding you back is you! Don't hide behind your fears and insecurities any longer. There is still a fight in your heart that wants to be on the battlefield. This fight is not just for you; it is for all those you love. Don't look back any longer, but look forward to the great victory that lies ahead of you. I will give you the same strength and courage I gave to King David over Goliath. All you have to do is be the one man who will to step out in faith in the midst of warfare and fight!

Your Lord,
Who Fights For You

"Together they will be like mighty warriors in battle trampling their enemy into the mud of the streets. They will fight because the LORD is with them, and they will put the enemy horsemen to shame."

Zechariah 10:5

_____

_____

_____

_____

_____

_____

_____

_____

_____

_____

_____

Prepare For Battle

My Warrior Son,
The time is now — get dressed for battle. I have not called you to a life of comfort. When you feel as if there is no fight left inside you, call Me and you will feel My spirit rise up inside your soul and give you strength. I alone hold the passion you need to persevere in any battle. I am your strength when you are week. In My power, you will conquer any spiritual giant that attempts to defeat you. Put on every piece of spiritual armor that I had given to you, and bury your heart in My word. Your life will not be wasted when you fight to further My kingdom. I have already given you the battle gear . . . now take it!

Your King,
Who Shields You

"He trains my hands for battle; He strengthens my arm to draw a bronze bow. You have given me Your shield of victory. Your right hand supports me; Your help has made me great."

Psalm 18:34

_____

_____

_____

_____

_____

_____

_____

_____

_____

_____

_____

_____

The Power of Prayer

My Warrior Son,

Never underestimate the power that I have given you in your prayers. You have the same power inside of you that I gave Elijah to call down fire from Heaven and reignite faith in hearts of man once again. There is an invisible war around you and your prayers will bring about evidence of my power at work in the world. I want you to confidently call on heaven that you may see My mighty hand move on earth. Your words spoken in someone's dark hour will move My spirit to light their path. Your prayer for the lost and lonely will usher in My Spirit to comfort them and send My angels to their aid. One day, on the other side of eternity, you will see how your prayers affected and protected many lives during your life.

Your God,
Who Loves When You Pray

"Then if My people who are called by My name will humble themselves and pray and seek My face and turn from their wicked ways, I will hear from Heaven and will forgive their sins and restore their land."

....

2 Chronicles 7:14 (NLT)

_____

_____

_____

_____

_____

_____

_____

_____

_____

_____

_____

_____

Fueled By Faith

My Warrior Son,
You no longer have to be controlled by circumstance. You can learn to live your life fueled by faith. What you see will cause you to lose hope. Your faith will free you from fear and give you the power to persevere under trail this life brings. If you have faith even as small as a mustard seed, I will move any mountain that stands in your way. With faith, nothing will be impossible for you to accomplish. However, I cannot force you to have faith in me. Only you can make the choice to believe. If you chose to stand on My word, then you will see My promises come to pass in and through you!

Your King,
Who Has Faith In You

"I tell you the truth, if you have faith as small as a mustard seed, you can say to this mountain, 'Move from here to there,' and it will move. Nothing will be impossible for you."

Mathew 17:20 (NIV)

_____

_____

_____

_____

_____

_____

_____

_____

_____

_____

_____

Run to Win

My Warrior Son,
It is time to commit to the call I have on your life by disciplining yourself spiritually the same way a great athlete trains to win a worldly race. I know what I ask of you is not easy. Your perseverance will make you the great man I created you to be and bring glory to Me. Don't waste your race running for the praises of people or you will lose your stamina and fall. You must run this race of faith keeping your eyes fixed on the eternal prize I will give you when you cross the finish line! You will never look back with regret if you let Me, your Life Coach, push you to your full potential! All who watched you run, will forever remember your race. You will do more than run; you will win!

Your Lord,
Your Life Coach

"Don't you realize that in a race everyone runs, but only one person gets the prize? So run to win! All athletes are disciplined in their training. They do it to win a prize that will fade away, but we do it for an eternal prize."

1 Corinthians 9:24-25 (NLT)

When Life Hits

My Warrior Son,
When life hits hard, I suffer with you. I, your Savior, know the burdens placed upon you. I have already carried them on My shoulders. In My darkest hour, I was alone and I cried to My Father for another way—a less painful way. Yet, I chose to walk this path of pain for you. Just as olives must be crushed to make oil, I poured out My life as a love offering for you. Don't give up your faith in these dark hours because there is powerful purpose in your suffering. I will not waste a single tear that you've shed. I hear your cry for help and I will come to your aid. I am your rock and rescuer, and I will deliver you!

Your Lord,
Who Suffers With You

"But in my distress I cried out to the Lord; Yes, I prayed to my God for help. He heard me from His sanctuary; My cry to Him reached His ears."

Psalms 18:6 NIV

Battlefield of the Mind

My Warrior Son,

It is critical that you shield your mind with the truth and be strategic about what you allow yourself to read, watch, and think. Your greatest fight is against your own thoughts. The enemy will try to invade your head with every sinful thought. His goal is to cripple your calling by setting a temptation trap for you to fall in. Do not allow the enemy's sensual weapons to destroy the man I destined you to be. Every evil deed is first constructed in the heart with one thought. Therefore, take every thought captive and run from whatever weakens your walk with Me. You can take control of your thoughts by immersing yourself in My word. Victory is yours . . . walk in it!

Your Savior,
Who Gives You Victory

"We demolish arguments and every pretension that sets itself up against the knowledge of God, and we take captive every thought to make it obedient to Christ."

....

2 Corinthians 10:5

_____

_____

_____

_____

_____

_____

_____

_____

_____

_____

_____

Truth Is Your Armor

My Warrior Son,
I know you live in a world that believes many lies. I have equipped you to fight the temptation to live a lie. You know who I am, and I am the truth. Anything that does not line up with My word is a lie. I want you to become radical for My truth. I know there will be times that truth will be a tough road traveled, however truth is the only road that keeps you free from walking in guilt and condemnation. It is only My truth that clears up confusion and helps the lost find their way to me. Live for My truth and reject the lies of the enemy so that you can be whole. Now throw off any lies that have been placed on you and discover the freedom that is yours to share!

Love Your King,
Who Is The Truth

"He will declare to his friends,' I sinned and twisted the truth, but it was not worth it. God rescued me from the grave, and now my life is filled with light."

Job 33:27-28 (NLT)

No Weapon Will Prosper

My Warrior Son,
This is not the time to surrender to the immoral war and wickedness of this world. You are much needed on the battlefield. No weapon formed against you can or will destroy you because you are Mine. You have the power in My name to demolish anything the devil uses to attack. You do not have to allow his blows to wipe you out any longer. Don't fight using the weapons of the world. Make up your mind to fight in My power and take authority where I have given you authority. This is your time, now take your shield of faith and use it to protect yourself and those who don't know how to protect themselves!

Your Commander & King,
Who Fights For You

"For though we live in the world, we do not wage war as the world does. The weapons we fight with are not the weapons of the world. On the contrary, they have divine power to demolish strongholds."

2 Corinthians 10:4 (NIV)

_____

_____

_____

_____

_____

_____

_____

_____

_____

_____

_____

BECOME FEARLESS

My Warrior Son,
Nothing can defeat you but you trying to fight in your own strength and wisdom. I have not given you the spirit of fear but of a sound mind. I have not called you to run away from the battles this life brings, but to face the giants in your life and conquer them! As long as you are walking in My power, truth, and you surrender your conflicts to me, you have nothing to be afraid of. Therefore, I call you "fearless" the way I called my chosen Gideon a Valiant Warrior, when he was afraid to fight. Do not be disheartened by what your natural eye sees. I am the same God that gave Gideon the power to overcome his countless enemies and I am fighting for you right now. So I command you now, as your King, do not fear!

Your God,
Who Demolishes Fear

"Do not be afraid of the terrors of the night, Nor the arrow that flies in the day. Do not dread the disease that stalks in darkness, nor the disaster that strikes at midday. Though a thousand fall at your side, though ten thousand are dying around you, these evils will not touch you."

Psalm 91:5-7

Courage to Change

My Warrior Son,

Real courage is exemplified when you willingly let go of who you are now so you can become who I have called you to be. Your courage to humble yourself and confess your sin to Me will become the key to your freedom. You will find something far greater than the temporary pleasures of living for this world; you will discover a powerful peace unlike anything this world has to offer. No one has the power to paralyze you from your purpose. I gave My life for you to have a better one. I will also give you the courage needed to walk away from the old ways and embrace your new life in Me. You are Mine, and I call you by name. Now take the power I have given to you and make a change!

Love Your King,
Your Courage

> "Therefore, if anyone is in Christ, he is a new creation; old things have passed away; behold, all things have become new."
>
> ....
>
> 2 Corinthians 5:17 (NKJV)

GET UP

My Warrior Son,

One of the greatest battles you may ever face is the fight to forgive yourself. Nothing can keep you down, because I have already forgiven you and empowered you to rise again no matter what you have done. I gave my disciple, Peter, the strength to get up from guilt of denying My Son, Jesus. I gave My appointed king, David, the grace to get up from the shame of committing adultery and murder. I gave my apostle, Paul, the mercy to get up from persecuting My disciples. I gave my warrior, Gideon, the courage to get up from his fears and lack of self-worth. Today I am asking you to receive whatever you need from Me and accept My forgiveness so you can get up and finish strong!

Your King,
Who Helps You Up Whenever You Fall

> "Even if godly people fall down seven times,
> they always get up."
>
> Proverbs 24:16

The Bait of Bitterness

My Warrior Son,
I know how hard it is to react righteously when feelings of anger and disappointment hit your heart. I, your Lord, have felt every emotion you feel when I walked the earth. I am not asking you not to feel anger, I am warning you not to give in to your anger and allow anyone to provoke you to compromise your character. Bitterness is the bait of satan. If you bite his bait and internalize your anger, you will become bitter. Nothing good can be birthed out of bitterness. Come to me as King David did, and pour out your angry heart to me. Under My authority, your anger will turn into Amazing Grace for those who have caused you pain.

Your Lord,
Who Knows How You Feel

"Refrain from anger and turn from wrath; do not fret, it leads only to evil. For evil men will be cut off, but those who hope in the Lord will inherit the land."

Psalm 37:8-9

SOVEREIGN SUFFERING

My Warrior Son,

I will allow trials and tribulation in your life to draw you closer to Me, strengthen you, and prepare you for battle. I prepared My chosen, King David, while he was running for his life and hiding in cave. I blinded My Apostle Paul until he was ready to see life through My sight. I allowed Job to lose everything so he would know that I am all He would ever need in this world. All the sovereign suffering of My chosen mighty warriors lead them to the purposeful life that I planned for them. Just as I was with Daniel in the lions' den, I am with you in every trial. You are being prepared for your purpose right now.

Your King,
Who Suffers With You

"Consider it pure joy, my brothers and sisters, whenever you face trials of many kinds, because you know that the testing of your faith produces perseverance. Let perseverance finish its work so that you may be mature and complete, not lacking anything."

....

James 1:2-4

_____

_____

_____

_____

_____

_____

_____

_____

_____

_____

_____

Spiritual Warfare

My Warrior Son,

Spiritual warfare is not a game; it is very real. Sometimes, when you feel your strength fading, you will need to run away from temptations to keep from falling. Running away may seem weak, but you must take radical measures to win this spiritual war. No temptation can conquer you if you get out while there is still time. The enemy will always try to tempt you to linger long enough to entangle you in sin. His strategy has taken down many great men of Mine. I will not allow you to be tempted more than you can handle. I will always make a way of escape. Only you can ultimately make the choice to take My exit and save yourself from heartache and regret.

Your King,
Your Great Escape

> "You are tempted in the same way that everyone else is tempted. But God can be trusted not to let you be tempted too much, and He will show you how to escape from your temptations."
>
> 1 Corinthians 10:13 (CEV)

Pick up Your Cross

My Warrior Son,
I have great and mighty works for you to conquer. Those works will only be accomplished if you are willing to deny yourself, your desires, and let go of everything and anything to follow Me and My desires. I know what I ask of you is not an easy choice to make. However, the benefits and blessing are great for those who lay down their own desires and dreams to live for me. Great men of Mine are not measured by how much they can pick up but rather by how much they can lay down. When you are ready to lay down your own life so someone else can live, you truly find the fullness of life!

Your Lord,
Who Gave His Life For You

> "He who does not take up his cross and follow Me is not worthy of Me. He who finds his life will lose it, and he who loses his life, for My sake, will find it."
>
> Matthew 10:38-39 (NKJV)

_____

_____

_____

_____

_____

_____

_____

_____

_____

_____

_____

_____

IDENTITY CRISIS

My Warrior Son,

Who do you say that I am? If I am your great and mighty God created in My image, then you are great and mighty also. If you believe that I am who I say I am, then you can believe that you are who I say you are. You need nothing from this world to prove your worth but a life lived for My glory—not your own. The praise of man is not enough to fill you up. It will leave you hollow, dry, and thirsty for something more. I am the one who will give you the satisfying self-assurance you are searching for. Lose yourself in Me. Take on My identity, and you will walk in an unshakable confidence and become completely secure.

Love Your King,
Who Defines You

"Out of all the people on the face of the earth, the Lord has chosen you to be His treasured possession."

Deuteronomy 14:2

Hopelessness is an Illusion

My Warrior Son,

Hopelessness is just an illusion. I am your hope and your mighty God. Just as I parted the Red Sea of hopelessness for Moses and My chosen people, I will part any sea that is blocking you from your freedom. You will walk in the promises I have for your life. Don't allow an illusion to become reality. The enemy's fires will not burn you out. Raging waters cannot drown your dreams. I am bigger than any challenge you are facing. Fight the temptations to give up and quit. I know the plans I have for you and they are not for harm but for your good. I am working on your behalf right now. You will get through this. Trust Me and watch My faithfulness be proven once again!

Your King,
Your Hope

"For I know the plans I have for you," says the Lord. "They are plans for good and not for disaster, to give you a future and a hope."

....

Jeremiah 29:11 (NLT)

STAND

My Warrior Son,

When you feel too beaten down to fight, I want you to give all that you have. Stand, be strong and courageous, and keep your faith no matter what hits. I have warned you that evil days will come. You may feel shaken and disoriented when the enemy assaults you, but I will supply you with the strength to withstand any punch. Even when everyone else around you has been burnt out and struck down by the pressure of battle, I want you to stand. Be the man who stands in the gap for those who cannot stand on their own! You wear My armor. You are fully equipped to remain strong until this spiritual war is finally over, and then we can celebrate your victories together!

Your King,
Who Stands In For You

"So put on all of God's armor. Evil days will come. But you will be able to stand up to anything. And after you have done everything you can, you will still be standing."

....

Ephesians 6:13

_____

_____

_____

_____

_____

_____

_____

_____

_____

_____

_____

Relational Wars

My Warrior Son,

Your fight is not against flesh and blood, but it is against spiritual forces of darkness. Therefore do not give into the relational wars. Do not drain your strength trying to prove your point, win your way, or defend yourself to another person. I am your defense. Do not engage; no one ever wins the blame game. You are called to live above a life of excuses. Defeat the enemy by fighting for the relationship and doing what you can to bring peace to the situation. The truth is, nothing anyone has said or done to you can stop My plans from coming to pass. Now, fight for the things worth fighting for—righteousness, salvation, and My name.

Your King,
Your Defense

"If it is possible, do all that you can to live in peace with everyone. Dear friends, never take revenge. Leave that to the righteous anger of God. For the Scriptures say, 'I will take revenge; I will pay them back,' says the Lord."

....

Romans 12:18-19

In the Dark

My Warrior Son,

I created you to be a light in the dark places of this world. Where light is, darkness cannot be. Today, I am asking you to choose the life I destined you to live. Give Me access to those dark hidden places in your heart and let My marvelous light penetrate through your inmost being. Nothing you have done can be hidden from Me. I give grace and want to eliminate the shame and guilt that you feel for what you have done in the darkness. Don't waste another day in shadows of shame; confess you sin to me—I am your redeemer. I will once again set you up as My light in this darkened world. It's time, My chosen one, to come clean and let your Savior set you free once again!

Your King,
Who Gave For Your Freedom

"Whatever you have said in the dark will be heard in the light, and what you have whispered behind closed doors will be shouted from the housetops for all to hear!"

Luke 12:3 (NLT)

Tender Warrior

My Warrior Son,

I call you "warrior" because I created you in My image. I captivated the world with My tender love and mercy when I walked the earth. I proved My love by serving My people to the point of dying on the cross. I called you to follow My lead, and I have prepared your heart to love as passionately as I have loved you. It is not enough to just fight for your faith. Your tender love for others will make you a true hero. I have given you the power to leave an indelible mark on the hearts of all who are close to you. When this life is over, all that will matter is that you loved well and finished strong!

Your King,
Who Loved You With His Life

> "Surround me with your tender mercies so I may live, for Your instructions are my delight."
>
> Psalm 119:77

A Time for War

My Warrior Son,

I have created a time for every season of life. There is My perfect timing for every plan I have. Right now there is a time of war upon you. The enemy's attacks are great. It is time for My people to put on my full armor and fight like never before. I know the battles you face will not be easy, but they will be worth fighting for. You will be fighting for your family and your children's children. Look around; you are much needed on the battlefield. Enlist your life in My mighty spiritual army, and you will not be defeated. There is nothing for you to fear for I am with you fighting for you. You will conquer and win souls for My kingdom.

Your King,
Who Has Already Won

> "To everything, there is a season: A time to love and a time to hate. A time for war and a time for peace."
>
> Ecclesiastes 3:8 (NLT)

Not Of This World

My Warrior Son,

You are not of this world; your soul will never be able to settle into this place because your citizenship is in heaven. I warn you as temporary residents to keep away from worldly desires that wage war against your very souls. Don't trade eternal rewards for a life of lust and luxury. I can provide more satisfaction for you than you could ever provide for yourself! Why waste your life storing up treasures here on this earth? I brought you into this life with nothing, and that is how you will leave. You will only find the significance you are searching for when you begin to invest your time and talent in the eternal things that will last. Store up your treasures in Heaven.

Your Lord,
The Builder Of Your Eternal Home In Heaven

"Jesus answered, 'My Kingdom is not an earthly kingdom. If it were, My followers would fight to keep Me from being handed over to the Jewish leaders. But My Kingdom is not of this world."

John 18:36 (NLT)

Rebuild What is Broken

My Warrior Son,

I have called you to look to the future with hope and rebuild what is broken. I am the same God who gave Nehemiah the strength and favor to rebuild the broken walls of Jerusalem, and I will give you the power and strength to do the same. Let me give you the tools to rebuild broken hearts with words of hope, and rebuild broken relationships with forgiveness and grace. Rebuild broken cities with selfless service, and rebuke the enemy's lies with words of truth. I will go before you and prepare the people for the mighty works that I will do through my Holy Spirit in you. Begin the building process today by laying one stone of good works at a time.

Your King,
The Master Builder

"But now I said to them, "You know very well what trouble we are in. Jerusalem lies in ruins, and its gates have been destroyed by fire. Let us rebuild the wall of Jerusalem and end this disgrace!"

....

Nehemiah 2:17

_____
_____
_____
_____
_____
_____
_____
_____
_____
_____
_____
_____

Rest Warrior

My Warrior Son,

I am your Creator and I created a day of rest for my people from the beginning. Rest is not an option; it is a command for My chosen ones. Even I, the God of the universe, took a Sabbath day. I know that you have much that you want to accomplish, but without restoration you will not have the strength to conquer much. Don't allow the cares of this world to cause you to become weak and weary. Come to Me and I will give you rest. Lay down your burdens and I will carry them. Rest is My gift to you to renew your strength and refresh your soul. Place your cares in My trustworthy hands and rest!

Your God,
Your Perfect Peace

"Jesus said, 'Come to Me all of you who are weary & carry heavy burdens, and I will give you rest.'"

Matthew 11:28

Conquer Evil

My Warrior Son,
The enemy will always try to persuade you to conquer evil with evil, but you will lose every time you give in to your anger and compromise your character. You never need to give into the temptation to conquer evil by responding with evil. That tactic is for the weak. Revenge brings nothing but pain, destruction, and regret. Love brings peace, healing, and My blessing. My spirit is in you therefore you have the inner strength to love at any cost. Your protection in the heat of battle is a pure heart that willingly prays for your enemies. Be extreme and love others most when they deserve it the least . . . The way I love you!

Your Lord,
Who Loved You With My Life

"Instead, If your enemies are hungry, feed them. If they are thirsty, give them something to drink. In doing this, you will heap burning coals of shame on their heads. Don't let evil conquer you, but conquer evil by doing good."

....

Romans 12:20-21 (NLT)

_____
_____
_____
_____
_____
_____
_____
_____
_____
_____
_____
_____

The Power of Purity

My Warrior Son,
It's time to purify yourself, so don't pretend to be pure. Be pure in your mind and your motives. With every temptation the enemy fires at you, there is a choice and it is a choice only you can make for yourself. You can cave to your craving for temporary pleasures and destroy your soul, or you can call to Me and I will make away for you to escape. I am a Holy God and I want you to live a life of holiness. I am not asking for perfection, I am asking for your purity to be a priority in your life. Remove from your path anything that causes you to stumble and fall away from Me. It is purity that will give you peace of mind and the power to effectively proclaim you are Mine. Your purity will bring My promises to pass in your life!

Your King,
Who Purifies You

> "Then Joshua told the people,
> 'Purify yourselves, for tomorrow the Lord
> will do great wonders among you.'"
>
> ....
>
> Joshua 3:5 (NLT)

_____

_____

_____

_____

_____

_____

_____

_____

_____

_____

_____

_____

Amazing Grace

My Warrior Son,

No matter where you've gone, what you have done, or what you have said, I have covered you with My blood. If you refuse to forgive yourself, you are saying My death on the cross was not enough to set you free from sin. At the cross, I covered your guilt, your shame, your regret, and your pain. I washed you clean with My blood. I cover you everyday with My extravagant love and mercy. My resurrecting power will give you the new life you long for, and My grace is a free gift. Now take the gift of grace I give to you, and give it away to those who have let you down or disappointed you! Amazing Grace is a reflection of My love for the world to see through you!

Your God,
Your Grace

> "But my life is worth nothing to me unless I use it for finishing the work assigned me by the Lord Jesus—the work of telling others the Good News about the wonderful grace of God."
>
> Acts 20:24 (NLT)

WOMEN

My Warrior Son,

I created a woman to complete a man. Yet, My beautiful creation has been used too many times by the enemy to cripple My great men like King David and Samson. Immoral women destroy the foundation I built for family. Too many of My mighty men have not guarded their hearts and minds and have fallen prey to the seduction of a woman. They have traded all they have worked for and all that I have done in their lives in a moment of weakness. Do not think you are strong enough to handle the seduction of a woman. Run from an immoral woman. You do not have to surrender to your sensual cravings. I can, and will, make a way for you to escape, but you must choose to take My way out!

Your Father,
Your Escape

"[the adulterous woman] Entering her house leads to death; it is the road to the grave. The man who visits her is doomed. He will never reach the paths of life. Follow the steps of good men instead, and stay on the paths of the righteous."

....

Proverbs 2:18-20

Praise through the Pain

My Warrior Son,
Pain is inevitable in this fallen world, but I have given you the strength to endure anything the enemy attempts to do to torment you. I can use hurtful situations to make you into the man I created you to be. I want you to learn to praise Me in pain and become a comfort to others. Your praise will become the keys to your freedom. Your praise will call down Heaven to earth, and I will move mightily in your life if you will praise Me during difficult times. If you trust Me, then you will praise Me until I come to your rescue. Just as I moved the earth to set the Apostle Paul free from prison, I will do what ever it takes for your freedom as well.

Your King,
Who Frees You

"Paul & Silas were praying & singing hymns to God, and the prisoners were listening to them. Suddenly, there was a great earthquake, so that the foundations of the prisons were shaken; and immediately all the doors were opened & everyone's chains were loosed."

....

Acts 16:25-26 (NKJV)

BORN TO LEAD

My Warrior Son,

You were born to lead. But only you can make the choice to step into your appointed position as a leader. You are called to raise the bar and bring others up and not allow them bring you down. No matter what choice you make, you will lead others by your example—good or bad! Your obedience to Me is the only weapon that will destroy the works of the enemy in your life. I am the same God who equipped Moses to lead My people out of captivity. I will go before you and prepare the way. In My power you will have the wisdom and influence needed to become a great leader. Now, walk in My confidence, not your own, and lead My people!

Your King,
Who Leads You

> "Now go, for I am sending you to Pharaoh. You must lead My people Israel out of Egypt."
>
> Exodus 3:10 (NLT)

The Trust Factor

My Warrior Son,

I ask you on this day, "Who do you trust?" There is a trust factor that will prove to the world how much faith you have in Me, your Lord. I am the author of your life and I am the giver of every breath you take. I want you to surrender all fear to Me and trust Me! I hold in My mighty hand all of your tomorrows. They were laid out before you were born. Give up the fight in your own mind of trying to figure it all out. Don't let your circumstance hold your heart hostage or cause you to lose your confidence in Me. I am asking you on this day to answer this one question,
"In whom do you place your trust?"

Your Trustworthy King,
Who Loves You

"So do not throw away this confident trust in the Lord. Remember the great reward it brings you! Patient endurance is what you need now, so that you will continue to do God's will.
Then you will receive all that He has promised."

....

Hebrews 10:35-36 (NLT)

_____
_____
_____
_____
_____
_____
_____
_____
_____
_____
_____

The Work Force

My Warrior Son,
I am the God who gave you the ability to work, and wherever you work is a part of your mission field. There is so much more to your job than profit and status. What do you profit if you gain everything and lose your soul? Wherever you stand is holy ground. Your work ethics are a reflection of Me. You are not your own. You were brought with a price. I have destined you for success. You do not have to give in to the work ethics of this world. Pursue a spirit of excellence in everything that you do. Do your work, as unto to Me, and in My time I will reward you greatly for glorifying Me in the work force!

Love Your God,
Whose Rewards Are Great

> "For God is not unjust to forget your work and labor of love which you have shown toward His name, in that you have ministered to the saints, and do minister."
>
> ....
>
> Hebrews 6:10

_____

_____

_____

_____

_____

_____

_____

_____

_____

_____

_____

_____

Breakthrough
(Life or Death)

My Warrior Son,

My love for you is unconditional but My blessings are not. It is your time to break free from mediocrity and break through to the life of abundant blessing and adventure. I have handed you the keys to unlock a life better than you could ever hope for. However, I will not force you to live for Me. Obedience is a choice only you can make. If you choose My will over your way, I will open the floodgates of Heaven for you. I will bless your obedience by prospering everything you lay your hands to do that brings glory to Me. Your obedient life will not only release My blessing and favor on you but also your family and many generations to follow.

Love Your King,
Your Blessing

"If you fully obey the Lord your God and carefully follow all His commands I give you today, the Lord your God will set you high above all the nations on earth. All these blessings will come on you and accompany you if you obey the Lord your God."

Deuteronomy 28 :1-2 (NIV)

_____
_____
_____
_____
_____
_____
_____
_____
_____
_____
_____

Driven by Eternity

My Warrior Son,
Live your life driven by eternity. Don't waste your days pouring your heart and soul into things that will not make an undying impact. Do not let your faith be shaken by a bad day, what is one day compared to eternity? Look at the big picture. If you will let the blaze of eternity burn in your heart, you will be more than a light in the darkness. Your faith will be a contagious fire that will spark the faith in many people all around you. Your life lived for Me will become a legacy that will still be effective in the hearts of man long after you're gone. Greatness is yours when eternity reigns on earth through you!

Your King,
Who Loves You For All Eternity

"Yet God has made everything beautiful for its own time. He has planted eternity in the human heart, but even so, people cannot see the whole scope of God's work from beginning to end."

Ecclesiastes 3:11 (NLT)

Conquer Compromise

My Warrior Son,

You never need to compromise your character to get ahead of the rest. I am the One who ultimately appoints promotion. You are set apart and called to live a life that reflects you are Mine. If you fully trust Me, you will find the strength to conquer compromise. What matters most to Me is what you do when only I am watching. I am the one who sees your heart. Your choice to walk with Me on the straight and narrow road will give you so much more than the wide road that leads to a life of dishonor and destruction. Now, live your life according to My standards not your own, and I will give you the desires of your heart.

Your King,
Who Does Not Compromise

"They do not compromise with evil, and they walk only in His paths. You have charged us to keep Your commandments carefully."

Psalm 119:3-4 (NLT)

Capture This Day

My Warrior Son,
Capture this day! The enemy of your soul wants to torment you with worry and fear of the future. This is a disruptive trap set by satan himself. Don't waste your strength today fighting to figure out tomorrow. If you take your eyes off today, you will grow too weary from all your worry. Don't you know by now that I hold all your tomorrows in my hand? I will never let you down. Today is My gift to you, now open it and live it passionately for Me. I am asking you on this day to be where you are and give all that you have! I want you to fast off worrying about your future and focus on your faith in Me.
Let this day be one well lived!

Love Your King,
Who Made This Day

"But seek first His kingdom & His righteousness,
and all these things will be given to you as well.
Therefore do not worry about tomorrow,
for tomorrow will worry about itself.
Each day has enough trouble of its own."

....

Matthew 6:33-34

_____

_____

_____

_____

_____

_____

_____

_____

_____

_____

_____

The Invisible War

My Warrior Son,
There are unseen spiritual battles going on all around you. Darkness wars against My chosen ones every day. You must learn to fight in the power of My spirit not your human flesh. I will give you every weapon needed to be an effective warrior. My Holy Spirit will be your sight when you cannot see the invisible attacks fired at you. Your faith in Me is your shield when you feel oppressed by the enemy and My word is your sword to strike down your opponents. Do not fear, My son, you are fully equipped to fight the good fight of your faith. I won't let you live a life of defeat; you can, and will, take authority over ever demon of darkness. I will give you the power to triumph over every trial.

Love You King,
Who Has Already Won

"For our struggle is not against flesh and blood, but against the rulers, against the authorities, against the powers of this dark world and against the spiritual forces of evil in the Heavenly realms."

Ephesians 6:12

_____
_____
_____
_____
_____
_____
_____
_____
_____
_____
_____
_____

POWERLESS APART FROM ME

My Warrior Son,

It doesn't matter how strong or fast you are on the outside, apart from Me you are powerless. You must learn to fight your enemy in My strength, not yours. I am inside you and I am your source of power. If you do not let My strength pulse through you then you will not win. Your enemy deceives you and he jabs at your weak spots but you can overtake Him in my authority, not yours. Be strong in your faith and fight with the weapon of My word and the power of prayer. Take control in the fighting ring by fighting for righteousness, not revenge! Don't sit down in weary defeat and don't go another round with the evil one in your own strength. Step back into to the ring and fight like the man of God I have trained you to be, and you will win!

Your Lord,
Your Victory

"I am the Lord all powerful so don't depend on your own strength but on My Spirit."

....

Zechariah. 4:6

_____
_____
_____
_____
_____
_____
_____
_____
_____
_____
_____
_____
_____

Blessed

My Warrior Son,

If you pay attention to the commands of your Lord, I will abundantly bless you for your obedient heart dedicated to Me. I, your Father in Heaven, want to bless when you come in and blessed when you go out. I will grant you victory over any enemies who rise up against you. You will not be defeated if you obey Me. I will send a blessing on your household and on everything you put your hand to. I will bless your children because you lived your according to My standards and not the world's. My favor will follow you wherever you go if you will walk with me. I will open Heaven's storehouse to you so you may bless others with all I give you. I will bless you with peace of mind and abundant prosperity for your faithfulness. Your life will be one well celebrated because you lived for Me!

Your King,
Your Blessing

"Praise the Lord. Blessed are those who fear the Lord, who find great delight in His commands. Their children will be mighty in the land; the generation of the upright will be blessed. Wealth and riches are in their houses, and their righteousness endures forever."

Psalm 112:1-3 (NIV)

_____
_____
_____
_____
_____
_____
_____
_____
_____
_____
_____

Release Your Prisoner

My Warrior Son,
Forgiveness is not an option; it is my command. I am a just God and I will deal with those who cause My people pain. Don't allow yourself to remain prisoner of self-defeat because of unforgiveness. I gave My life for your freedom. Take the keys and unlock the prison door that is holding your heart hostage. You can't fight the good fight of faith with heavy chains of bitterness and unforgiveness on your feet. Refusing to forgive is not hurting or hindering anyone but you. Lay down your heavy heart of unforgiveness at My cross and feel your chains fall to the ground. When you release your prisoner, you release yourself!

Love Your King,
Who Has Forgiven You

"Even if that person wrongs you seven times a day and each time turns again and asks forgiveness, you must forgive."

....

Luke 17:4 (NLT)

Count the Cost

My Warrior Son,

You must count the cost of any and all commitments you make before you make them. Opportunities that may appear good could become a trap set by the enemy to capture your time and talent. Remember, there is a way that seems right to man but in the end leads to destruction. You are of great value weather you believe it or not. I paid a big price for your life therefore I want you to spend your time wisely. Take a few days to pray and seek Me and I will reveal what is right for you. Don't allow anyone but Me to move you into a position that requires your time and attention. I am your navigator in this life. Never let anyone guilt you to go where I have not mapped out for you.

Your King,
Who Paid The Price For You

"Don't trap yourself by making a rash promise to God and only later counting the cost."

....

Proverbs 20:25 (NLT)

Never Underestimate

My Warrior Son,

Nothing is impossible for Me. All I ask is that you be faithful in the little things. I am your faithful Father who will move mountains for you if you even have faith in Me as small as a mustard seed. I am the One who multiplied two fish and a loaf of bread to feed my children. I sent My Son into the world in the form of a little baby. Greatness begins with the little things in you do to glorify Me. I bless whatever you give Me no matter how big or small. Test Me, that I will not pour out a blessing too big for you to contain. Begin your faith walk with the little things and expect to see big miracles begin to happen in your life!

Your Lord,
Who Holds Nothing Back

"You don't have enough faith," Jesus told them. "I tell you the truth, if you had faith even as small as a mustard seed, you could say to this mountain, 'Move from here to there,' and it would move. Nothing would be impossible."

....

Matthew 17:20 (NLT)

Take Your Appointed Position

My Warrior Son,

Just as I appointed My chosen one Daniel to a high position and gave him many valuable gifts, I, your King, have appointed you as well. Your character and commitment will place you in your true appointed position. There is a hope and a future for you but only you can capture it by seeking My face with all your heart, mind, and strength! There is a Call on your life but only you can answer it. Your appointed position is for My glory not your own. You must chose for yourself if you will settle for less than I offer. Now is your time to take your rightful place as a man of faith and change lives for eternity!

Your King,
Who Appointed You

"Then the king appointed Daniel to a high position and gave him many valuable gifts. He made Daniel ruler over the whole province of Babylon, as well as chief over all his wise men."

Daniel 2:48 (NLT)

Life without Limits

My Warrior Son,

You have My spirit inside of you therefore you have My power to live a life without limits. There is no war I cannot win for you. There is no problem I cannot solve for you. There is no life too broken that I cannot put back together again. There are no chains strong enough that I cannot break. Don't ever doubt who you are in me. Nothing can limit you from living an abundant life but your disobedience and lack of faith. Chose to obey my commands and you will feel My power and passion resurrect inside your soul. I will do immeasurably more than you would ever dare to ask of Me or imagine!

Your King,
Who Knows No Limits

> "Now to Him who is able to do immeasurably more than all we ask or imagine, according to His power that is at work within us."
>
> Ephesians 3:20 (NIV)

Wisdom of a Warrior

My Warrior Son,

Deception is a dangerous weapon launched by the enemy to keep the world from finding My truth. But I, your God, will give you access to a greater device: "The Weapon of Wisdom" empowered by My Holy Spirit! I want you to hunt for My wisdom as if your life depends on it; because it does! When you discover how to use the weaponry of My word, you will break down walls and destroy the deceptive works of the enemy. My wisdom will become your guard, your guide, and your gauge to navigate your way through the battlefield. My wisdom will give you the skills to rebuild and restore many broken lives including your own. If you get lost in My word, you will never be blinded by deception again.

Love Your King,
Who Freely Gives Wisdom

"For the Lord gives wisdom, and from His mouth come knowledge and understanding. He holds victory in store for the upright, He is a shield to those whose walk is blameless, for He guards the course of the just and protects the way of His faithful ones."

Proverbs 2:6-8 (NIV)

Speak Life!

My Warrior Son,

Today and everyday you have a choice to make: you can speak life to yourself and others or you can speak death. Your tongue is a powerful weapon; with it you build others up or tear them down. You can bring peace or war with your words. You can speak with compassion or you can crush someone's spirit. I have anointed your tongue to counteract the enemy's verbal attacks on you and My church. I have chosen you to be My voice of comfort and courage to the world. Your words can deliver hope to the hopeless and life-changing truth to those lost in lies. Let your words be a blessing not a curse, and let them be a reflection of Me every time you open your mouth to speak!

Love Your King,
Who Is Life

> "I will watch what I do and not sin in what I say. I will hold my tongue when the ungodly are around me."
>
> ....
>
> Psalm 39:1

The Legacy

My Warrior Son,

Your life lived for Me will become the legacy that lives on long after you are gone. Your fight will never be forgotten. You are a hero of the faith and your commitment to the call will crave character in the next generation. Every prayer you prayed will become a blessing passed down. Every tough choice you made to obey Me will become a foundation of faith your family will stand on in their tough times.

Your courage will continue to bring comfort to many during their difficult times. Your trust in Me will remain in others who watched you walk in peace. I, your God, declare on this day that your children's children will be forever blessed because you lived your life for an audience of one . . . Me!

Love Your King,
Who Believes In You

"Their children will be successful everywhere; an entire generation of godly people will be blessed. They themselves will be wealthy, and their good deeds will never be forgotten."

Psalm 112:1-3

It is Finished!

My Warrior Son,

It is finished. I, your savior, paid the price for your eternal life when I drew My last breath on the cross. I conquered death, I covered your sin with my blood, and I crushed the enemy. Now, My spirit is in you to finish the work you have been sent to do. My power is yours to use. My keys to freedom are now yours to share. My grace is your gift to receive. All regret or guilt is gone and the new has come; because it is finished. Never doubt how much you are loved. I proved it on the cross. Now, walk in the truth. It is finished and you will finish strong!

Love Your King,
Who Loves You More Than You Can Imagine

"When He had received the drink, Jesus said,
'It is finished.'
With that, He bowed His head and gave up His spirit."

John 19:30 (TNIV)

For More Ministry & Books

with Sheri Rose

HisRoyalFamily.com

Made in the USA
Coppell, TX
02 December 2021